LUCY: THE AUSTRALOPITHECUS THAT FELL OUT OF THE HUMAN EVOLUTION TREE

Daniel A. Biddle, Ph.D.

 GENESIS apologetics

www.genesisapologetics.com
A 501(c)(3) ministry equipping youth pastors, parents, and students with Biblical answers for evolutionary teaching in public schools.

LUCY: THE AUSTRALOPITHECUS THAT FELL OUT OF THE HUMAN EVOLUTION TREE
by Daniel A. Biddle, Ph.D.
Printed in the United States of America

ISBN-13: 978-1543174724

ISBN-10: 1543174728

Dedication

To my wife, Jenny, who supports me in this work. To my children Makaela, Alyssa, Matthew, and Amanda, and to your children and your children's children for a hundred generations—this book is for all of you.

We would like to acknowledge Answers in Genesis (*www.answersingenesis.org*), the Institute for Creation Research (*www.icr.org*), and Creation Ministries International (*www.creation.com*). Much of the content herein has been drawn from (and is meant to be in alignment with) these Biblical Creation ministries.

"Guard what has been entrusted to you, avoiding worldly and empty chatter and the opposing arguments of what is falsely called 'knowledge'—which some have professed and thus gone astray from the faith. Grace be with you."
—1 Tim. 6:20–21

"This is the Lord's doing; it is marvelous in our eyes."
—Psalm 118:23

Contents

About the Author

Dr. Daniel A. Biddle is president of Genesis Apologetics, Inc., a 501(c)(3) organization dedicated to equipping youth pastors, parents, and students with Biblical answers for evolutionary teaching in public schools. Daniel has trained thousands of students in Biblical Creation and evolution and is the author of several Creation-related publications. Daniel also serves as the Vice Chairman of the Board of The International Association for Creation, a non-profit ministry serving to unify the Biblical Creation movement. Daniel's experience and qualification in the secular realm includes a Ph.D. in Organizational Psychology from Alliant University in San Francisco, California, an M.A. in Organizational Psychology from Alliant, and a B.S. in Organizational Behavior from the University of San Francisco. Daniel has worked as an expert consultant and/or witness in over 100 state and federal cases in the areas of research methodologies and analysis.

About Genesis Apologetics

Genesis Apologetics is a non-profit 501(c)(3) ministry that equips Christian students and their parents with faith-building materials that reaffirm a Biblical Creation worldview. We are committed to providing Christian families with Biblically- and scientifically-based answers to the evolutionary theory that many children are taught in public schools. Our doctrinal position on Biblical Creation aligns with Answers in Genesis and the Institute for Creation Research (ICR), two of the largest Creation Apologetic Ministries in the U.S.

Readers are encouraged to view our free training resources at *www.debunkevolution.com,* *www.genesisapologetics.com* and our YouTube Channel (Channel Name: Genesis Apologetics).

Introduction

Reading through a 6th grade World History textbook might lead the reader to believe that there are thousands of examples of humanlike creatures that lead up to modern humans. **But do you know that you could fit all of the bones that supposedly prove human evolution into a pickup truck?**[1]

According to Biblical Creation, God made Adam and Eve only about six thousand years ago, and all human varieties—living and extinct—descend from the original couple. According to evolution, death of "less fit" apes into humans over millions of years. We cannot rewind time to view firsthand the creation of mankind, but we have lots of evidence supporting creation. Unfortunately, school textbooks don't mention this evidence.

If the Bible is true, God created us supernaturally, a reason exists for our creation, and we will eventually answer to God for how we lived our lives. On the other hand, if public school textbooks are correct and natural processes made us, we have no lasting purpose, and will not be held accountable to a Creator after this life. Think about it—if you believe that humans evolved from apes, then why not just live like you want to live? Without a God, there is no "good," no "evil," and no basic moral laws like the Ten Commandments to guide your life. In this view, there would be no afterlife, no judgment, and no accountability after you die! However, if we believe in a God who made us on purpose, we have meaning, significance, and accountability in this life, and a hope for everlasting life. Knowing where we came from gives us a firm foundation for daily decisions and even everlasting decisions. This is not just a side issue. It impacts every area of our lives.

A Quick-Tour Through Human Evolution Icons

Key icons have carried the idea that humans evolved from ape-like creatures beginning millions of years ago. However, these iconic fossils fit categories like "extinct ape," "extinct human variety," and "hoax," but none of them fit the imaginary "ape-like ancestor" category. Let's briefly look at just three of the most famous icons that have been used over just this last century: Piltdown Man, Nebraska Man, and Neanderthals.

Piltdown Man

Piltdown Man was a main icon of human evolution from 1912 to 1953, over 40 years. He was even given the scientific name *Eoanthropus dawsoni*, and over 500 books[2] and papers were written about this icon. Then, in 1953, the truth came out that the whole thing was a fraud, being made of a doctored ape jaw and human skull, both artificially stained to look old.[3] Nonetheless, Piltdown Man received a lot of press, and was even credited by the New York Times as "proving" Darwin's Theory of Evolution! (see Figure 1)

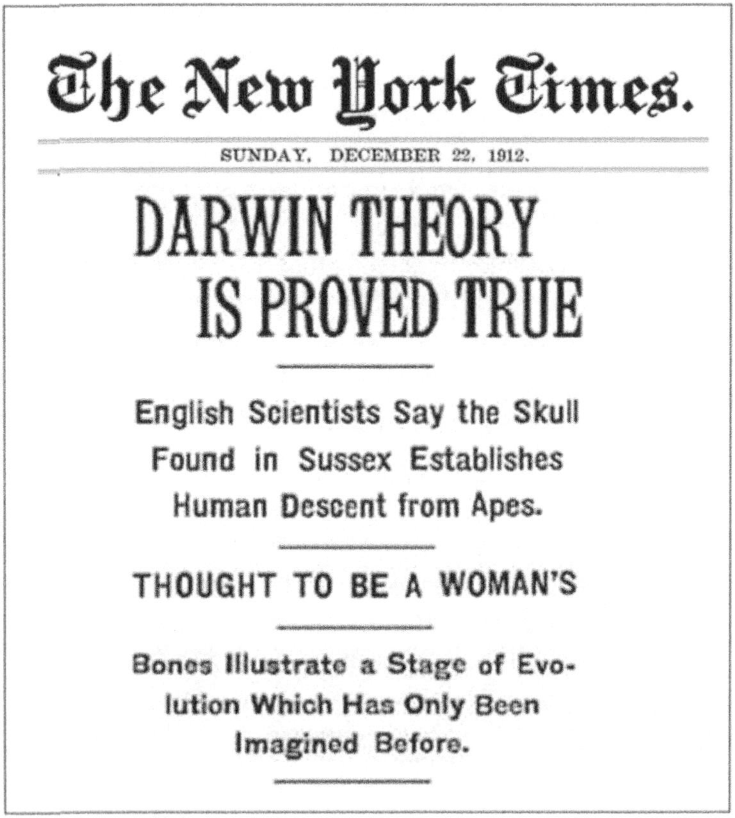
The New York Times.

SUNDAY, DECEMBER 22, 1912.

DARWIN THEORY IS PROVED TRUE

English Scientists Say the Skull Found in Sussex Establishes Human Descent from Apes.

THOUGHT TO BE A WOMAN'S

Bones Illustrate a Stage of Evolution Which Has Only Been Imagined Before.

Figure 1. Piltdown Man Announced in the New York Times (1912).[4]

In 1915, Sir Arthur Keith, Conservator of the Royal Medical College in England and President of the Royal Anthropological Institute of Great Britain and Ireland in the early 1900s, wrote the most definitive human evolution text of that era, *The Antiquity of Man*.[5] This 500+ page book prominently displayed a gold embossed skull of the Piltdown Man.

Over 100 pages of Arthur Keith's *The Antiquity of Man* book[6] is devoted to Piltdown Man, which was revealed as a fraud just two years before Keith died in 1955.[7] Keith placed so much trust in Piltdown Man as a "proof of evolution" that he called it: "one of the most remarkable discoveries of the twentieth century."[8] Boy was he wrong! But it was too late. He had convinced his readers that human evolution had scientific backing, when it never did.

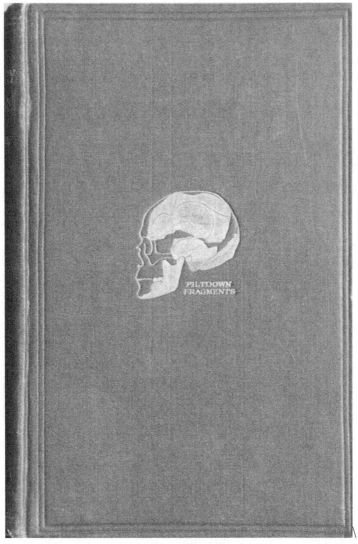

Figure 2. Sir Arthur Keith's Leading Human Evolution Book of the Early 1900s with Piltdown Man on the Cover.[9]

Historians continue to investigate who did it and why. A 2016 report showed evidence that Charles Dawson performed the forgery by himself. In any case, Piltdown Man was a hoax.[10]

Nebraska Man

From 1917 to 1928, yet another icon dominated the scene as "certain proof" of human evolution. Geologist Harold Cook found a ***single molar tooth*** in Nebraska which later was named *Hesperopithecus haroldcooki*, or Nebraska Man.

Figure 3. Nebraska Man[11]

In 1922, the head of the American Museum of Natural History (Henry Fairfield Osborn) proclaimed that the single molar found by Harold J. Cook in 1917 belonged to the first *pithecanthropoid* (ape-man) of the Americas, hence the name "western ape." The globally-distributed *Illustrated London News* broadcast British evolutionist Grafton Elliot Smith's receiving knighthood for his efforts in publicizing Nebraska

Man. This imaginative "reconstruction" of the tooth's owner is a club-carrying ape-man walking upright. It shows primitive tools, possibly domesticated animals, and a brutish bride gathering roots. An artist derived all this from a single tooth! In July 1925, the Nebraska Man tooth was used to prove man evolved from ape-like creatures in the Scopes "Monkey Trial" held in Dayton, Tennessee.

This all changed when excavations continued in 1927–1928 at the same place the tooth was found. These excavations revealed that the tooth belonged neither to man nor ape, but to a wild pig![12] Then, in 1972, living herds of this same pig were discovered in Paraguay, South America.[13] According to the late renowned creation scientist Duane T. Gish, "this is a case in which a scientist made a man out of a pig, and then the pig made a monkey out of the scientist!"[14] "Nebraska man" turned out to be another hoax.

Neanderthals

Neanderthals were used to promote the idea of human evolution for over 120 years, and most people over 40 today will remember them widely used in textbooks as the ancient, half-ape, half-human brutes that "modern humans" supposedly evolved from. But over the last few decades, researchers have finally recognized fully human features in Neanderthal burials. They buried their dead, made musical instruments, tools, cosmetics, jewelry, and purses. Recent DNA sequence comparisons even confirm that they interbred with humans! While they had some differences in size and shape compared to people today, they were most certainly just people. Neanderthals represent extinct varieties of mankind, much in the same way that mammoths represent extinct varieties of the elephant kind.

Figures 4 and 5 show this changing position on Neanderthals—from pre-human "brute" to human.

Figure 4. Previous Idea of Neanderthal Man (published in *L'Illustration and in the Illustrated London News* in 1909).[15]

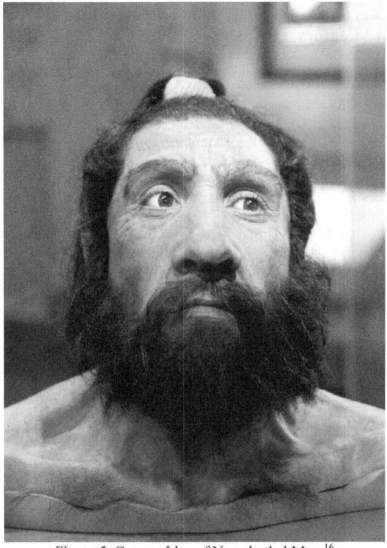

Figure 5. Current Idea of Neanderthal Man.[16]

Once considered an ape-like caveman, Neanderthal remains have proven their identity as fully human. Give him a shave, haircut, and button-down shirt and this Neanderthal would blend right into a city crowd.

17

Lucy: The Leading Human Evolution Icon of the 21st Century

See our Lucy Video: *www.genesisapologetics.com/lucy/*

Now we turn to the leading human evolutionary icon of today: Lucy. The year 1974 welcomed the famous "Lucy," a fossil form that bears the name *Australopithecus afarensis*. Lucy is arguably the most famous human evolution icon ever displayed in public school textbooks. Pictures and dioramas of Lucy inhabit countless museums and thousands of articles and dissertations.

Donald Johanson discovered Lucy in Ethiopia, Africa, and she quickly grew to be known as the supposed "missing link" between man and ape. At only about 3-1/2 feet tall and only about 60 pounds, she's very close to the size of small apes today.[17] The scientific name *Australopithecus* simply means "southern ape." Southern ape is a very appropriate name because, as you'll learn below, Lucy was just that—an ape!

Although public school textbooks often state that Lucy was our ancestor and they feature human-like drawings of her, the fossil evidence tells quite a different story. Over 40 years of Lucy research and about 20 more discoveries of her kind have raised new questions about its supposed evolutionary connection. Evolutionary research journals have substantiated ten fatal flaws regarding the claim that Lucy and her species are really our early ancestors.[18]

Fatal Flaw #1: Lucy's Skull

Even though only a few fragments of Lucy's skull were found, they revealed that her skull was about the same size as a chimpanzee. As Donald Johanson himself said, "Her skull was almost entirely missing. So knowing the exact size of Lucy's brain was the crucial bit of missing evidence. But from the few skull fragments we had, it looked surprisingly small."[19] Later estimates reveal that Lucy's brain was just one third the size of a human brain, which makes Lucy's brain the same size as the average chimpanze brain.[20]

Sir Solly Zuckerman, chief scientific advisor to the British government, said that the "*Australopithecine* skull is in fact so overwhelmingly ape-like, as opposed to human that the contrary position could be equated to an assertion that black is white."[21]

The skull in Figure 6 shows a rendition of what Lucy's skull may have looked like. Notice that the brown parts are what they found; the white parts used to fill in most of the skull are imagined. Notice its sloped and ape-like. It's also the size and shape that closely resembles a modern bonobo (a cousin to the chimp).

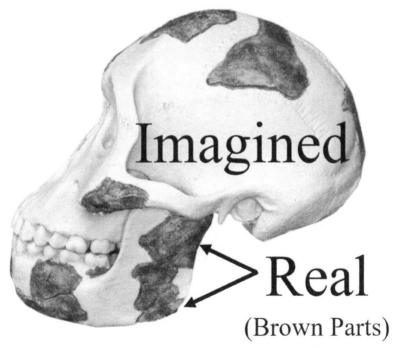

Figure 6. Lucy's Skull Reconstruction.[22]

Leading paleontologist, Dr. Leakey, stated, "Lucy's skull was so incomplete that most of it was 'imagination made of plaster of Paris,' thus making it impossible to draw any firm conclusion about what species she belonged to."

The Foramen Magnum

The foramen magnum is a hole in the bottom of a skull where the top of the spinal cord enters. The angle at which the spinal cord entered the foramen magnum of Lucy's species is nearly identical to a chimp's—indicating that Lucy's species walked hunched-over on all fours.[23]

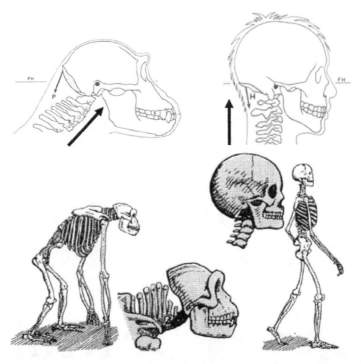

Figure 7. Foramen Magnum Angle and Walking Angle Comparison (Chimps to Humans).[24]

One study conducted by evolutionary scientists showed that the angle of the foraman magnum of Lucy's species was "well below the range for our sample of modern humans but overlaps the low end of the range for position between modern apes and humans, but closer to the former (chimpanzees, specifically)."[25]

Fatal Flaw #2: Lucy's Semicircular Canals

Humans have three semicircular canals embedded deep within our ears that are integrated with our brains, heads, and eyes to keep us balanced as we move. Apes' semicircular canals orient to their up-tilted heads. To investigate how these semicircular canals are involved in the movement of various creatures, scientists have studied them in depth using advanced scanning techniques and making measurements of their different structures. *Australopithecines*, as well as other living and non-living apes, all have semicircular canals that fit ape-oriented heads that fit bodies designed for walking on all fours, whereas humans semicircular canals match upright, two legged locomotion.

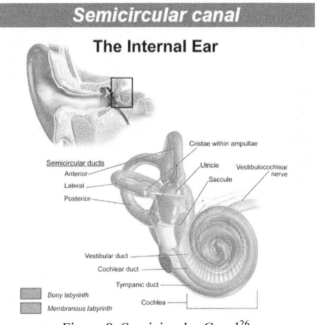

Figure 8. Semicircular Canal[26]

In particular, they learned that the semicircular canals of *Australopithecines* were best suited for "facultative bipedalism,"[27] which means walking occasionally on two feet, just like many apes walk today. While this study focused on *Australopithecus africanus*—and Lucy's species has been labeled *Australopithecus afarensis*—they are anatomically similar.[28]

What about Lucy's species specifically? Dr. Bernard Wood conducted a study that revealed that the semicircular canals of Lucy's species "were more like those of chimpanzees than of modern humans. The fluid-filled semicircular canals are crucial in maintaining balance, and so all three lines of evidence suggest that the locomotion of *Australopithecus afarensis* was *unlikely to have been restricted to walking on two feet*"[29] (emphasis added).

Another report in the leading secular science journal *Scientific American*[30] reviewed the research conducted on a baby *Australopithecus afarensis*, stating: "Using computed tomographic imaging, the team was able to glimpse her semicircular canal system, which is important for maintaining balance. The researchers determined that the infant's semicircular canals resemble those of African apes and other *Australopithecines* (such as *Australopithecus africanus*). This, they suggest, could indicate the *Australopithecus afarensis* was not as fast and agile on two legs as we modern humans are."

One fascinating aspect of semicircular canals is that, while they all work together, each of them provides a separate sense of directional balance: "The superior canal detects head rotations on the anterior-posterior (side-to-side movement, like tilting the head toward the shoulders) axis. The posterior canal detects rotations on the sagittal plane (forward and backward movement, like sit-ups). The horizontal canal senses movement on a vertical basis, as the head rotates up-and-down on the neck."[31]

It just so happens that the two same canals that are most involved for helping us walk upright are the two canals that are *statistically significantly different*[32] between humans and chimps. Lucy's species clearly identifies with chimps. Dr. Spoor noted that two of the three semicircular canals in particular coordinate "upright bipedal behavior" because they are involved in "movements in the vertical plane" (i.e., upright walking). [33] Drs. Day and Fitzpatrick agree with this, stating: "The anterior and posterior canals of the human vestibular organs are enlarged in size relative to the horizontal canal whereas the three canals are more equal in size in other species. The significance of this is that the anterior and posterior canals are orientated to sense rotation in the vertical planes, *the movements that are important for controlling upright balance*"[34] (emphasis added).

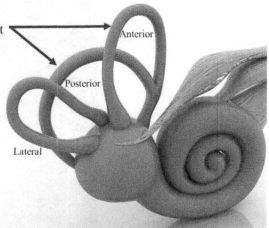

These two are most associated with upright walking, and they are significantly different between apes/Lucy's species and humans.

Anterior

Posterior

Lateral

Figure 9. Semicircular Canals[35]

What difference does this make? Well, think about it this way: If you had your semicircular canals surgically replaced with a chimp's, at the very least, you'd be really disoriented! Your head would feel level only when you were looking to the sky. You wouldn't be able to run with as much ease as you have now, since the same two semicircular canals that are significantly different between apes and humans help stabilize your head when running.[36]

Fatal Flaw #3: Lucy's Mystery Vertebra

In 2015, press releases started coming out and showing that, even after 40 years of study involving hundreds of scientists, one of Lucy's bones (a vertebra) didn't even belong to her![37] In fact, it didn't even belong to Lucy's species, but was from a *Theropithecus*, a type of baboon. Does that make you wonder if we're really dealing with bones from a single individual with Lucy? Especially when Lucy was put together from hundreds of bone fragments that were found scattered along a hillside?[38]

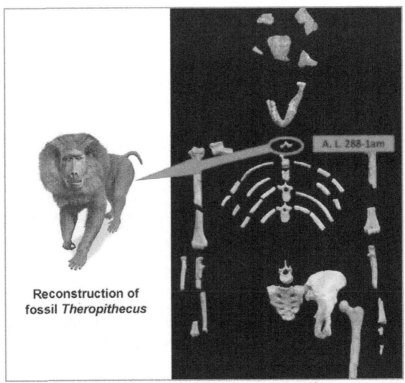

Reconstruction of fossil *Theropithecus*

A. L. 288-1am

Figure 10. Lucy's "Extra" Vertebra.[39]

Fatal Flaw #4: Lucy's Pelvis

Next, we have Lucy's pelvis, which Johanson's team believed was "broken apart and then fused together during later fossilization..." which caused it to "be in an anatomically impossible position" and to "flare out like a chimp's pelvis."[40]

Their solution to this problem was to use a power saw to cut it apart and then piece it back together! After "fixing" the pelvis, they noted: "It was a tricky job, but after taking the kink out of the pelvis, it all fit together perfectly, like a three-dimensional jigsaw puzzle. As a result, the angle of the hip looks nothing like a chimp's, but a lot like ours..."[41]

Even secular scientists who hold to evolution have problems with Lucy's pelvis reconstruction, stating "We think that the reconstruction overestimates the width of this [pelvis] area, creating a very human-like sacral plane,"[42] and another stated, "The fact that the anterior portion of the iliac blade faces

laterally in humans but not in chimpanzees is obvious. The marked resemblance of AL 288-1 [Lucy] to the chimpanzee is equally obvious."[43] Charles Oxnard, evolutionist and author of the *Order of Man*, stated that her bones seemed to show that she was a "real swinger... based on anatomical data, *Australopithecines* must have been arboreal [tree-dwelling] ... Lucy's pelvis shows a flare that is better suited for climbing than for walking."[44] Isn't it interesting how these remarks from evolutionary scientists never make their way into public school textbooks? Instead, Lucy is typically shown walking upright, as shown in Figure 11.

Figure 11. Lucy in Public School Textbooks.[45]

Fatal Flaw #5: Lucy's Locking Wrists

Lucy had locking wrists like quadruped apes, not like humans.[46] This has been widely reported in both scientific journals as well as the general media. For example, even the *San Diego Union Tribune* reported, "A chance discovery made by looking at a cast of the bones of 'Lucy,' the most famous fossil of *Australopithecus afarensis*, shows her wrist was stiff, like a chimpanzee's, Brian Richmond and David Strait of George Washington University in Washington, D.C., reported. This suggests that her ancestors walked on their knuckles."[47] The study conducted by these scientists concluded: "Measurements of the shape of wristbones (distal radius) showed that Lucy's type were knuckle walkers, similar to gorillas."[48]

When interviewed about their study (published in *Nature*) they stated: "It suddenly occurred to me that paleoanthropologists had never looked at the wrists of Lucy or other important early human ancestors discovered since the early papers were published...." so while they were visiting the Smithsonian, they went to the cast collection, inspected Lucy's radius [forearm bone], and found that she had the "classic knuckle-walking feature." This became obvious when they "saw a ridge of bone on the lower forearm that prevented Lucy's wrist, like that of a chimpanzee or gorilla, from rocking backward, but allowed it to lock in an upright position for easy knuckle-walking."[49] Figure 12 highlights this "locking wrist" feature they found on Lucy's bones.

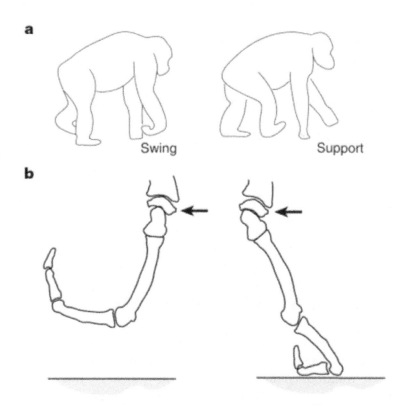

Figure 12. Lucy's Locking Wrist.[50]

The study conducted by Richmond and Strait revealed that Lucy had the same concave arm bone that joined with her convex wrist, creating a locking system that allowed for both swinging and stable knuckle-walking (as shown in Figure 13).

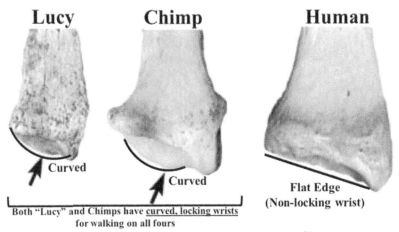

Figure 13. Lucy's Locking Wrist.[51]

Figure 13 shows a close-up view from the study. The arm bone on the far left is from Lucy; the one in the middle is from a chimp; and the one on the far right is human. Notice how Lucy's bone is matches the chimp's—they both have the concave shape that allows the wrist to lock into place for knuckle walking. Humans do not have any angle for this whatsoever because we're not designed for walking on our hands!

Fatal Flaw #6: Lucy's Curved Fingers

Next, we'll take a look at the fingers of Lucy's species. Comparison of various apes, humans, and Lucy's species' finger curvatures reveal some major differences. Even evolutionary scientists have admitted that the curved fingers of Lucy's species were best suited for swinging in trees.[52] One study statistically compared various finger measurements from several different types of apes against humans, and grouped the fingers of Lucy's species in the same category as chimps and bonobos, and far away from human's straight fingers (see Figures 14 and 15).

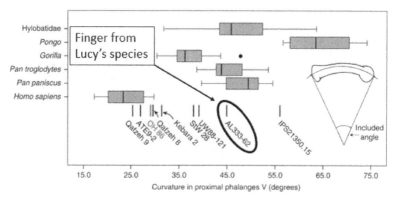

Figure 14. Finger Curvature Study Revealing Lucy's Species Is Categorized with Apes and Gorillas.[53]

Figure 15 shows a finger from one of Lucy's species, showing significant curvature compared to human fingers, which are not curved.

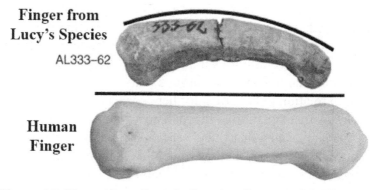

Figure 15. Finger from Lucy's Species Compared to Human Finger.[54]

Other examples of *Australopithecine* apes had curved fingers and ape-like limb proportions that point toward her kind as living in trees, so the same was probably true of Lucy.[55]

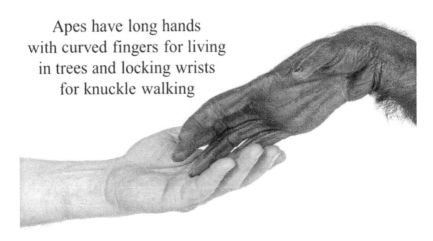

Apes have long hands
with curved fingers for living
in trees and locking wrists
for knuckle walking

Figure 16. Human and Chimp Hands.

Fatal Flaw #7: Lucy's Short Little Legs

Some evolutionary scientists have argued that Lucy's legs were much too short for upright walking. Some say she walked with a "bent-hip, bent-knee" method; some say she might have "shuffled"; some say she walked on all fours; some say she was bipedal. For example, Dr. Bill Jungers at the Stony Brook Institute in New York argued that "Lucy's legs were too short, in relation to her arms, for her species to have achieved a fully modern adaptation to bipedalism."[56] Drs. Stern and Sussman advocated that Lucy's species would have walked "bent-hip, bent-knee" method, much like a living chimpanzee, because of the number of skeletal features in their skeletons which are functionally associated with arboreality in living apes (e.g., curved phalanges, long trunk but short legs, etc.).[57] Dr. Hunt argued that the most efficient behavior for Lucy's species would have been "bipedal posture augmented with bipedal shuffling" as a consequence of anatomical compromise between the needs of terrestrial bipedality and arboreal climbing.[58]

Without any of Lucy's species alive today, one cannot know for certain how they moved around. But that hasn't stopped several scientists—from both the evolution and creation camps—from speculating about it. As we have reviewed in this section, however, plenty of evidence *from evolutionary scientists* indicates she likely walked on all fours (including her semicircular canals, skull, locking wrists, curved fingers, and now, her short legs).

Fatal Flaw #8: The Widespread Exaggeration of Lucy's Human-like Appearance

Lucy was originally found in *hundreds* of pieces before she was painstakingly glued together in the way they believed she was before she died. Even though many of the first reports that came out after Lucy was discovered stated that Lucy's skeleton was "40% complete,"[59] Lucy's discoverer (Johanson) clarified this in a book published 22 years after Lucy was found, stating: "Lucy's skeleton consists of some 47 out of 207 bones, including parts of upper and lower limbs, the backbone, ribs and the pelvis. With the exception of the mandible [lower jaw] the skull is represented only by five vault fragments, and most of the hand and foot bones are missing."[60] This computes to actually **23%** of the complete skeleton (47 ÷ 206), not "about 40%."

Numerous artists have drawn Lucy with human feet even though the fossil lacked both hand and foot bones. Frustratingly for those who care about truth, these illustrations continue to ignore subsequent finds, revealing that *Australopithecines* had curved ape fingers and grasping ape feet. Figure 17 shows how Lucy is represented at public exhibits, such as those found at the St. Louis Zoo and Denver Museum of Nature and Science.

Figure 17. Lucy at Public Exhibits (Zoos and Museums). Lucy at the St. Louis Zoo (Left) and at the Denver Museum of Nature and Science (Right).[61]

Most Lucy models show her with white sclera of the eye visible, even though 100% of all apes alive today have eyes that look dark because the sclera is not visible. Do you think this was done to make her look more human-like?

It's amazing how they can find hundreds of bone fragments scattered across a hillside in a nine-foot radius[62] that supposedly lay in the soil for over 3 million years and reconstruct a human-like Lucy, complete with eyewhites displayed in museums around the world! At least one bone belonging to a completely different animal was mistaken for Lucy's for over 40 years. Were there others?

Figure 18. Making Lucy Look Human from Hundreds of Bones Fragments, Glue, and Imagination.

To further exaggerate Lucy's human-like appearance, some Lucy models don't even have hair! (see Figure 19).

Figure 19. Hairless Lucy Walking with her "Family," including Incorrect (Human) Feet and Hands. [63]

33

Fatal Flaw #9: Gender

A great deal of debate has emerged even over Lucy's gender, with some scientists arguing that the evidence shows she was actually a male! Articles with catchy titles have emerged such as "Lucy or Lucifer?[64] and more recently, "Lucy or Brucey?"[65] If evolutionists are so certain that we evolved from Lucy-like creatures, but they can't seem to even determine the gender of the leading human evolution icon, what other assumptions are being made?

Fatal Flaw #10: Falling out of a Tree to Her Death

Now we move onto the most recent news about Lucy. In 2016 the University of Texas had a team of orthopedic surgeons reveal the findings of a study that evaluated the numerous "compression" and "greenstick" fractures in Lucy's skeleton. A greenstick fracture goes by this name because it's the type of bone break that occurs under compression or fast bending—much like a green stick would break when such force is applied.

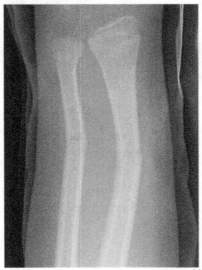

Figure 20. Greenstick Fracture[66]

This team determined that Lucy most likely died while falling 40 feet out of a tree traveling 35 miles per hour, and was "conscious when she reached the ground" because of the way she tried to break her fall. Even the lead study scientist, John Kappelman, remarks, "It is ironic that the fossil at the center of a debate about the role of arborealism (living in trees) in human evolution likely died from injuries suffered from a fall out of a tree."[67] Yes, it is quite ironic that Lucy, the supposed human ancestor who walked on two feet, died while falling 40 feet out of a tree.

But they've even offered a "rescuing device," stating that "because Lucy was both terrestrial and arboreal, features that permitted her to move efficiently on the ground may have compromised her ability to climb trees, predisposing her species to more frequent falls." So, to save the embarrassment of the "bipedal ape" dying by falling out of a tree, they believe that she must have fallen out of a tree because she wasn't used to living in them anymore." That's quite a reach for a creature that supposedly lived over 3 million years ago!

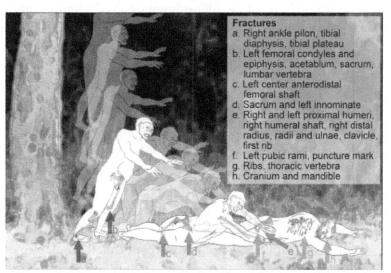

Figure 21. Lucy, the Supposedly Bipedal Ape, Falling 40-Feet from a Tree to Her Death.[68]

Lucy Summary

In summary, consider these conclusions about Lucy that were drawn from leading evolutionary scientists:

- Dr. Charles Oxnard (professor of anatomy) wrote, "The *Australopithecines* known over the last several decades ... are now irrevocably removed from a place in the evolution of human bipedalism ... All this should make us wonder about the usual presentation of human evolution in introductory textbooks."[69]
- Dr. Solly Zuckerman heads the Department of Anatomy of the University of Birmingham in England and is a scientific adviser to the highest level of the British government. He studied Australopithecus fossils for 15 years with a team of scientists and concluded, "They are just apes."[70]
- Dr. Wray Herbert admits that his fellow paleoanthropologists "compare the pygmy chimpanzee to 'Lucy,' one of the oldest hominid fossils known, and finds the similarities striking. They are almost identical in body size, in stature and in brain size."[71]
- Dr. Albert W. Mehlert said, "the evidence... makes it overwhelmingly likely that Lucy was no more than a variety of pygmy chimpanzee, and walked the same way (awkwardly upright on occasions, but mostly quadrupedal). The 'evidence' for the alleged transformation from ape to man is extremely unconvincing."[72]
- Marvin Lubenow, Creation researcher and author of the book *Bones of Contention,* wrote, "There are no fossils of Australopithecus or of any other primate stock in the proper time period to serve as evolutionary ancestors to humans. *As far as we can tell from the fossil record,*

36

when humans first appear in the fossil record they are already human"[73] (emphasis added).

- Drs. DeWitt Steele and Gregory Parker concluded: "Australopithecus can probably be dismissed [from human evolution] as a type of extinct chimpanzee."[74]

In reality, the remains of these ape-like creatures occur in small-scale deposits that rest on top of broadly extending flood deposits. They were probably fossilized after Noah's Flood, during the Ice Age, when tremendous rains and residual volcanic explosions buried Ice Age creatures.[75] Answers in Genesis provides a rendition of what Lucy most likely looked like (Figure 22).

Figure 22. What Lucy Most Likely Looked Like (Credit: Answers in Genesis Presentation Library).

Evolution vs. God: What's Wrong with the Idea That God Used Evolution to Create Everything (Theistic Evolution)?

In a nutshell, theistic evolution is the belief that God used biological evolution as the process to bring about the variety of life on Earth over millions of years. The Bible plainly disagrees with theistic evolution. In fact, they are opposites, as will be shown below.

More and more student-aged Christians are becoming theistic evolutionists—especially those who are raised in public school and don't receive much biblical training at home or in church.

One of the most common testimonies we hear from high schoolers goes something like this: They become Christians at a young age, but they don't get much training in doctrine, especially creation-evolution related topics. After being saturated in public school evolutionary teaching (and not hearing the Biblical Creation view from parents or church leaders), they start developing *cognitive dissonance*—the tension that develops when holding two contradictory beliefs. They begin questioning: "I know that God exists, but they seem to present so much credible evidence for evolution at school, and it seems like the 'smart scientists' tend to believe it." Many take the shortest route to resolving this mental tension by adopting a worldview that is somewhere between their Christian faith and evolution. Without even knowing it, they have just adopted the view of theistic evolution.

In one subtle play, the enemy has replaced their belief in an all-powerful God who spoke creation into existence over six days and His inerrant Word with a "god" who creates life through a process of death and suffering. If true, the Bible wouldn't really mean what it says! While some might believe there's nothing wrong with this belief, we'll challenge that perspective next by reviewing the six fatal flaws with theistic evolution.

The Six Fatal Flaws of Theistic Evolution

We've distilled the major problems of theistic evolution into a list of the top six. As we'll see, the problems with theistic evolution are not just some abstract theological problems—they bring a serious impact in the daily lives of believers. After all, our beliefs form the roots of our actions and the sum of our actions make up our lives and our choices.

Adam Versus Apes: Theistic Evolution Denies the Biblical Creation of Adam and Makes Apes Our Ancestors

The Bible is clear that Adam was made spontaneously and supernaturally by God, in God's own image and likeness, out of the dust of the Earth (Genesis 1:26 and following). We are not made in the image of some lower ape-like creature, and the "image" of God and His "likeness" does not match that of an ape.

Making this idea even worse, evolution would have humans shaped as we are today only because our particular line of ape-like ancestors out-lasted and even out-killed other varieties. This is a far cry from humans being specially created out of the dust of the Earth in the image of a loving and intentional God. Jesus Himself clearly disagreed with the ideas that millions of years of human evolution occurred by stating, "But from the *beginning* of the creation, God 'made them male and female'" (Mark 10:6) (emphasis added).

Biblical Order of Creation

The basic order of the Creation account in Genesis 1 disagrees with the modern theory of how evolution supposedly unfolded from the formation of the universe to life on Earth (see Table 1).

Table 1. Differences between the Bible and Evolution.

Bible	Evolution
Earth before the sun	**Sun** before the earth
Oceans before land	**Land** before oceans
Land plants first	**Oceanlife** first
Fish before insects	**Insects** before fish
Plants before sun	**Sun** before plants
Birds before reptiles	**Reptiles** before birds
God created man instantly after all other animals were created	The **process of death** created man, and evolution is still occuring, though invisible because it takes millions of years

Table 1 clearly lays out how the Biblical order of Creation is opposite to how evolution supposedly happened.

Theistic Evolution Makes Death, and not God, Our Creator

No matter which "version" of evolution one holds to—whether naturalistic evolution without a God, or theistic evolution with a process started by God and left to run its course, or progressive creation where God uses cosmological and geological evolution while occasionally wiping out and creating new life forms along the way—the core problem is that the process of *death is setup as the creator of life.*

Each of these versions of evolution has a bloody, competitive, "survival of the fittest" process as the creator of new life forms. Each starts from lower life forms and eventually leads to man over millions of years. There are some serious problems with this view, and it could not differ more from the biblical account! What kind of all-powerful God would need to use a cruel, experimental process to bring about the variety of life on earth?

The idea of *punctuated equilibrium* (a view even held, in some form, by many progressive creationists) holds that God advances evolutionary development by isolated episodes of rapid speciation between long periods of little or no change. In other words, God used "random, wasteful, inefficiencies" to create the world into which Adam was placed.[76] God didn't get it right the first time, so He had to experiment through a cruel random process as a means to advance new life forms?

To the contrary, the Bible holds that God initially created everything perfect, and then our sin initiated the process of death, suffering, and bloodshed. How could God look upon all His Creation and call it "very good" (Genesis 1:31) if animals (and later humans) were tearing each other apart to survive...for millions of years before Adam? Why would an all-powerful, loving, merciful God need to use a blood-filled, clumsy, random process to populate the Earth with animal variety? God's initial Creation was perfect, but we messed it up!

Yes, we see natural selection and survival of the fittest going on in today's world, but this process is a "mindless" one without creative agency. For example, consider a large field with a healthy population of grasshoppers in two color varieties, green and yellow. When the fields are green in the springtime, the green grasshoppers may thrive more than the yellow ones because they blend in to their surroundings, being less visible to their predators. Then, in the fall when the fields turn yellow, this process is reversed, and the yellow grasshoppers thrive. Is this natural selection producing new species? Certainly not! Rather, the pre-programmed gene variability that God installed into the grasshoppers interacts with their environment. The grasshoppers are all still grasshoppers! We see the same principle in oscillating bird beak shapes in Darwin's finches which are proudly used to promote evolution in today's school textbooks.

Theistic Evolution Places Death before Sin

Perhaps the most serious problem with theistic evolution is that it has man coming on the scene after billions of years of death-filled evolution has taken place. This makes the brutal "survival of the fittest" process God's idea instead of the consequence of sin. To the contrary, according to the Bible,

41

when man appears in Creation, he is perfect and sinless and there's no such thing as death. Death does not come into the picture *until man sins* ("but of the tree of the knowledge of good and evil you shall not eat, for in the day that you eat of it you shall surely die," Genesis 2:17). So, you can't have death of mankind before the Fall of man and have a logical foundation for the Gospel (see also Romans 5:12 and 1 Corinthians 15:22).

In addition to God clearly warning Adam that "death will come" if he sins, two stark truths in Genesis address this important "death before sin" topic.

First, animals did not eat each other at the beginning of Creation, and thus there was no "survival of the fittest" or "natural selection" process that could supposedly work to drive evolution forward. Humans and animals originally ate vegetation:

> And God said, 'See, I have given you every herb
> that yields seed which is on the face of all the
> earth, and every tree whose fruit yields seed; to
> you it shall be for food. Also, to every beast of
> the earth, to every bird of the air, and to
> everything that creeps on the earth, in which
> there is life, I have given every green herb for
> food' (Genesis 1:29–30).

God did not endorse humans using animals as a food source until *after* the Flood: "Everything that lives and moves about will be food for you. *Just as I gave you the green plants, I now give you everything*" (Genesis 9:3, emphasis added). Further, it seems that God put the fear of man into animals *after* the Flood because they would be a food source from that point forward: "And the fear of you and the dread of you shall be on every beast of the earth, on every bird of the air, on all that move on the earth, and on all the fish of the sea" (Genesis 9:2).

Second, how could God look over the billions of years of blood-filled "survival of the fittest" evolution until it finally reached man and then call Creation "very good" (Genesis

42

1:31)? This would make Adam's sin and the curse of death meaningless, because death had already existed for millennia! If death was used to create Adam and Eve, what was the real consequence of sin?

Figure 23. Is this a "very good" creation? Carnivorism entered the world after sin.

God's original creation was perfect. The first chapter of Genesis states six times that what God had made was "good" and the seventh time that "God saw everything that He had made, and indeed it was *very* good" (Genesis 1:31). Now, however, we can look at the world around us and see there has been an obvious change. Many animals live by predation. Lions eat their prey while still alive. Bears eat young deer shortly after they are born.

If God created a perfect world at the beginning and animals were first designed as vegetarians, how did these defense and attack structures (like fangs and claws) come about? There are two primary perspectives on this topic, so we'll briefly review each.

The first is that these features were not originally used for carnivorism. In other words, the design was the same but the function was different. Take sharp teeth, for example. Panda bears have incredibly sharp teeth, but 99% of their diet is bamboo.[77] The same is true for numerous other creatures that appear to be vicious meat-eaters, but have a primarily vegetarian diet.

Figure 24. Pandas eat bamboo, but have teeth structures that appear to be designed as a "meat-eater."

Vicious-looking canine teeth aren't just used for carnivorism, they are also used in communication. For example, many apes, dogs, cats, and other animals expose their canines to express dominance, ownership of mates, and guard territory. The same teeth that are used by wolves for killing and eating are used by dogs today for eating domestic dog food. Even sharp claws that are used today for predation are used in many cases for climbing and defense. So, this first view avoids suggesting that God's initial design features were intended to be harmful to other creatures in His creation.

One of the limitations with this first viewpoint is that it excludes animals from changes that the Fall certainly introduced to the other parts of Creation, such as thorns and thistles being introduced to plants. Genesis 3:17–19 is clear that plants were cursed by man's Fall with thorns and thistles, and plants use thorns primarily as a defense mechanism. Were animals exempt from similar changes that were introduced by the Fall?

The second viewpoint is that defense and attack features were introduced by God as a result of the Fall. However, it is not a widely-held Biblical Creation position that animals quickly and recently developed all physical features used for predation. This is because physical change was not required to make plant-eaters into meat-eaters; it was merely a change in *behavior*, as many of the features that are useful today for predation are also useful for eating plants. It is also interesting to note that many predators have to learn to kill, as many "social predators" (e.g., lions) are not born with the knowledge of how to hunt and kill—they are behaviors that are learned from the other animals in their group.

Let's apply these two viewpoints on one of the most "obviously carnivorous" animals of all time—*Smilodon*, the saber-toothed cat. Named after its scissor-like front teeth (some over six inches in length), this massive lion looks like a perfect killing machine. In fact, the two massive teeth even lack lateral (side to side) motion that would be necessary if it were a vegetarian. Biblical Creationist and Biologist, Dr. Nathaniel Jeanson addresses this challenge by stating:

> How did these big cats acquire their sharp teeth? At the Curse, God probably didn't speak sharp teeth into existence out of nothing. His acts of global creation were finished by day seven of the creation week (Genesis 2:1–3; Exodus 20:11; Hebrews 4:3). So where did the lion's teeth come from? ... God may have created creatures with latent genetic information to be "switched on" only after Genesis 3, a concept similar to the "mediated design" model. Alternatively, God may have created anatomical and physiological features capable of multiple purposes. Powerful jaws, now used to kill and tear flesh, may have

45

initially been used to open fruits and plant seeds of the size and hardness of modern watermelons and coconuts. Could the lion's teeth have been used for tearing tough plants and roots in the beginning? Biblically, this latter hypothesis is compelling. Consider the effects of the reversal of the Curse in Isaiah 11:6–7: 'The wolf also shall dwell with the lamb, and the leopard shall lie down with the kid; and the calf and the young lion and the fatling together...*the lion shall eat straw like the ox*.' In reversing the Curse, God doesn't seem to change the lion's anatomy; He simply changes the lion's behavior. Furthermore, Scripture explicitly mentions God switching the mental states of animals after the Flood (Genesis 9:2). Might He also have done something much like this at the Curse?[78] (emphasis added)

The Believer Loses the Power That Comes from Fully Believing in God's Word

Put simply, there is power that comes from fully believing in the Word of God. A straight-forward reading of the Bible's account of origins as laid out in Genesis 1 and 5 and Exodus 20:11—without spin or interpreting it through man's lens of "science"—will lead an honest reader to six days of Creation just thousands of years ago. If God really used evolution to create everything, He could have simply told Moses to write it down that way! But He didn't, and the Creation account reads much differently than how it might read if evolution took place over millions of years. The Bible is clear in several places that God "spoke" creation into existence.

Compromising on God's Word by agreeing with theistic evolution robs the Christian of the power that comes from standing fully on the Word of God, and claiming its authority. When Dr. Charles Jackson with Creation Truth Foundation was asked, "Do you meet many Christians at college who are drifting away from the faith?" his response was eye-opening:

> They're more than being drifted away from the faith; there's a current that's created under them that pulls them away from the faith. When you put a question mark after any Bible verses that don't have them there already (or verses that give a disclaimer like, 'this is a mystery'), like 'in six days the Lord God created heaven and earth and all that's in them' (Exodus 20:11), instantly you have a quantum drop in the joy and power of the Christian walk—all of the gifts of God in you—you can feel it. It's like someone pulled the plug and you are running on battery now, and a low battery at that. [79]

There is a close association between the Word of God and the Power of God (Hebrews 4:12, 6:5; Matthew 22:29). Can a Christian live a power-filled life and walk in God's will while denying the Word of God? Christians will live a more power-filled life when they strongly align what they believe and how they live to the Word of God. Every stanza of Psalm 119 mentions the Word in some way for this reason.

Denying God's special creation and not believing that He created the world by His Word (Hebrews 11:3; Psalm 33:6) creates a deep crack in the foundation of a Christian, even in ways that are sometimes not known by the person doubting. John Macarthur[80] adds to this discussing by stating:

> Christians will get out there, saying "Boy, we're against abortion, and we're against homosexuality, and we're against Jack Kevorkian because he's murdering people, and we're against euthanasia, and we're against genocide and, you know, we're against the moral evils of our society, etc." Why are we against

those things? Can you tell me why? Why are we against those things? Give me one reason. Here it is, because they're forbidden in Scripture. Is that not true? The only reason we're against abortion is because God's against it. How do we know that? Because it's in the Word of God. The reason we're against homosexuality, adultery, etc. is because of the Bible. You see, we stand on the Scripture. But the problem is we don't want to stand on the Scripture in Genesis. So we equivocate on whether or not the Bible is an authority at all. What do you think the watching world thinks about our commitment to Scripture? Pretty selective, isn't it?

Theistic Evolution Has Christ Dying for the Sins of a Mythical Adam

The genealogies in Genesis 5 and 10 and Luke 3 lead directly back to Adam, the first man created by God. But if these genealogies don't lead back to a real Adam who actually sinned, then who do they lead back to? Because the "sinner" Adam and the Savior Jesus are linked together in Romans 5:16–18, any theological view which mythologizes Adam undermines the biblical basis of Jesus' work of redemption.

Conclusion

When showing a Christian friend some of the design differences between apes and humans, he remarked "It's just so obvious that apes and humans were created differently by God! Why would you need to point that out to anyone?" That's a good question. If anyone opens their eyes and just looks around at the varieties of apes living today and the variability within humans, it's quite obvious that they are animals and humans are humans—with each reproducing "after their kind" just as forecasted by the Bible. There are no creatures living today that are between apes and humans, neither were there in the past. All that exists that "proves" evolution today is a pickup truck full of miscellaneous old bones that scientists desiring to believe in evolution have assembled in a story that "proves" it.

The stretches that are made about Lucy—trying so hard to make the bones fit the progressing line to humans—show just how much these faith-abandoning "scientists" want to leave behind the obvious creative acts of God and replace it with a self-assuring story of evolution they believe will get them off the hook from having to answer to an Almighty God after they die. It's both disturbing and sad.

Further, how is it that 96% of state education systems require evolution to be taught as fact, while 70% of Americans are "Christian" and 46% believe that God recently (and miraculously) created humans? Does that make any practical sense? Can you think of any other topic where half the population believes something about the past (like our origins) but almost all of educational systems teach the opposite? Surely this is true only in one area: our origins, including the questions of whether God exists and whether He has revealed Himself to us through history.

So what *is* going on with this topic in America? What explanation can make sense of all of this? Fortunately, the Bible gives us some clues. First, the Bible is clear that the *systems* of the world are under the "sway" or "control" of the enemy (1

John 5:19: "We know that we are of God, and the whole world lies under the sway of the wicked one"). We also know that in the end times a "strong delusion" will come that will lead people astray from God: "And for this reason God will send them strong delusion, that they should believe the lie, that they all may be condemned who did not believe the truth but had pleasure in unrighteousness" (2 Thessalonians 2:11–12). 2 Peter 3:3–6 also confirms that in the last days people will abandon the idea of the spontaneous supernatural creative and catastrophic acts of God, and use this philosophy to deny His sudden return.

All of this points back to the spiritual battle for our souls. The great lie of evolution convinces people there is no God and this will result in many entering eternity without Him. That's why this battle must be fought by each Christian, but in *sensitive and tactful ways*. Just ask an atheist friend what they think of "Bible believing fundamentalists." You will find that Christians have not done a good job at lovingly presenting the Truth. Rather, the reputations that Christians have developed is one where we are known for what we are *against*, rather than what we are *for*.

Sadly, this is quite the turn off to many seekers. Realize that walking up to a typical atheist and trying to convince them that God spontaneously created all life on earth just thousands of years ago will likely be too much to stomach—especially when they've received a lifetime of "millions of years of evolution" from almost every school, museum, and state park they've ever visited. This is why relationship building and prayer is so important. Once someone comes to faith, the "scales" will fall off of their eyes and they will be spiritually open to the truth about Creation.

But don't take this tact too far. Some hold to a strict "Jesus before Genesis" philosophy of evangelism, but in many cases, answering questions about Genesis is necessary *before* people will consider Jesus. When trying to "convert" the philosophical Greeks (who were culturally very similar to many people today), Paul first started with the fact that we are created by a loving God (Acts 17:26–27: "And He has made from one

50

blood every nation of men to dwell on all the face of the earth, and has determined their pre-appointed times and the boundaries of their dwellings, so that they should seek the Lord, in the hope that they might grope for Him and find Him, though He is not far from each one of us"). Many people will likely want to explore the evidence for Biblical Creation (over the evolutionary alternative) before going further down the road towards becoming a Christian, and that's exactly why we wrote this book.

To equip students for the specific evolution-based arguments they are presented in public school, we recommend our six-lesson, video based "Debunk Evolution" program, which can be downloaded free (*www.debunkevolution.com*) or purchased in hard copy from our website (*www.genesisapologetics.com*).

Praise the Lord from the heavens; praise Him in the heights! Praise Him, all His angels; praise Him, all His hosts! Praise Him, sun and moon; praise Him, all you stars of light! Praise Him, you heavens of heavens, and you waters above the heavens! Let them praise the name of the Lord, *for He commanded and they were created*.
—Psalms 148:1–5

Helpful Resources

The following websites are recommended for further research:

- Genesis Apologetics: *www.genesisapologetics.com*
- Debunking Evolution: *www.debunkevolution.com*
  Answers in Genesis: *www.answersingenesis.org*
- Answers in Genesis (High School Biology): *www.evolutionexposed.com*
- Creation Ministries International: *www.cmi.org*
- Creation Today: *www.creationtoday.org*
- Creation Wiki: *www.creationwiki.org*
- Evolution: The Grand Experiment with by Dr. Carl Werner: *www.thegrandexperiment.com*
- The Institute for Creation Research: *www.ICR.org*

Prayer of Salvation

You're not here by accident—God *loves* you and He *knows* who you are like no one else. His Word says:

Lord, You have searched me and known me.
You know my sitting down and my rising up;
you understand my thought afar off. You
comprehend my path and my lying down, and
are acquainted with all my ways. For there is not
a word on my tongue, but behold, O Lord, You
know it altogether. You have hedged me behind
and before, and laid Your hand upon me. Such
knowledge is too wonderful for me; It is high, I
cannot attain it. (Psalm 139:1–6)

God loves you with an everlasting love, and with a love that can cover all of your transgressions—all that you have ever done wrong. But you have to repent of those sins and trust the Lord Jesus Christ for forgiveness. Your past is in the past. He wants to give you a new future and new hope.

But starting this new journey requires a step—a step of faith. God has already reached out to you as far as He can. By giving His son to die for your sins on the Cross, He's done everything He can to reach out to you. The next step is yours to take, and this step requires faith to receive His son into your heart. It also requires repentance (turning away) from your past sins–a surrendered heart that is willing to reject a sinful lifestyle. Many believers have a much easier time leaving sinful lifestyles after they fully trust Jesus and nobody else and nothing else. Along with forgiveness, the Holy Spirit enters your life when you receive Jesus, and He will lead you into a different lifestyle and way—a way that will lead to blessing, joy, patient endurance under trials, and eternal life.

If you are ready to receive Him, then you would recognize these key Biblical truths.[81]

1. Acknowledge that your sin separates you from God. The Bible describes sin in many ways. Most simply, sin is our failure to measure up to God's holiness and His righteous standards. We sin by things we do, choices we make, attitudes we show, and thoughts we entertain. We also sin when we fail to do right things or even think right thoughts. The Bible also says that all people are sinners: "there is none righteous, not even one." No matter how good we try to be, none of us does right things all the time. The Bible is clear, "For all have sinned and come short of the glory of God" (Romans 3:23).

2. Our sins demand punishment—the punishment of death and separation from God. However, because of His great love, God sent His only Son Jesus to die for our sins: "God demonstrates His own love for us in this: While we were still sinners, Christ died for us" (Romans 5:8). For you to come to God you have to get rid of your sin problem. But, in our own strength, not one of us can do this! You can't make yourself right with God by being a better person. Only God can rescue us from our sins. He is willing to do this not because of anything you can offer Him, but **just because He loves you!** "He saved us, not because of righteous things we had done, but because of His mercy" (Titus 3:5).

3. It's only God's grace that allows you to come to Him— not your efforts to "clean up your life" or work your way to Heaven. You can't earn it. It's a free gift: "For it is by grace you have been saved, through faith—and this not from yourselves, it is the gift of God—not by works, so that no one can boast" (Ephesians 2:8–9).

4. For you to come to God, the penalty for your sin must be paid. God's gift to you is His son, Jesus, who paid the debt for you when He died on the Cross. "For the wages of sin is death, but the gift of God is eternal life in Jesus Christ our Lord" (Romans 6:23). God brought Jesus

back from the dead. He provided the way for you to have a personal relationship with Him through Jesus.

When we realize how deeply our sin grieves the heart of God and how desperately we need a Savior, we are ready to receive God's offer of salvation. To admit we are sinners means turning away from our sin and selfishness and turning to follow Jesus. The Bible word for this is "repentance"—to change our thinking to acknowledge how grievous sin is, so our thinking is in line with God's.

All that's left for you to do is to accept the gift that Jesus is holding out for you right now: "If you confess with your mouth, 'Jesus is Lord,' and believe in your heart that God raised him from the dead, you will be saved. For it is with your heart that you believe and are justified, and it is with your mouth that you confess and are saved" (Romans 10:9–10). God says that if you believe in His son, Jesus, you can live forever with Him in glory: "For God so loved the world that He gave his one and only Son, that whoever believes in him shall not perish, but have eternal life" (John 3:16).

Are you ready to accept the gift of eternal life that Jesus is offering you right now? Let's review what this commitment involves:

- I acknowledge I am a sinner in need of a Savior. I repent or turn away from my sin.
- I believe in my heart that God raised Jesus from the dead. I trust that Jesus paid the full penalty for my sins.
- I confess Jesus as my Lord and my God. I surrender control of my life to Jesus.
- I receive Jesus as my Savior forever. I accept that God has done for me and in me what He promised.

If it is your sincere desire to receive Jesus into your heart as your personal Lord and Savior, then talk to God from your heart. Here's a suggested prayer:

Lord Jesus, I know that I am a sinner and I do not deserve eternal life. But, I believe You died and rose from the grave to make me a new creation and to prepare me to dwell in your presence forever. Jesus, come into my life, take control of my life, forgive my sins and save me. I am now placing my trust in You alone for my salvation and I accept your free gift of eternal life.

If you've prayed this prayer, it's important that you take these three next steps: First, go tell another Christian! Second, get plugged into a local church. Third, begin reading your Bible every day (we suggest starting with the book of John). Welcome to God's forever family!

Endnotes

[1] Ian Tattersall, the Director of the American Museum of Natural History: "You could fit it all into the back of a pickup truck if you didn't mind how much you jumbled everything up." Bill Bryson, *A Short History of Nearly Everything* (London: Black Swan Publishing, 2004), 529.

[2] *Nature* Volume 274, #4419 (July 10, 1954): 61–62.

[3] Pat Shipman, "On the Trail of the Piltdown Fraudsters," *New Scientist*, 128 (October 6, 1990): 52.

[4] Image Credit: *http://up.botstudent.net/piltdown-man-new-york-times.jpg*

[5] Arthur Keith, *The Antiquity of Man* (London: Williams & Norgate, 1915).

[6] Arthur Keith, *The Antiquity of Man* (Philadelphia: J. B. Lippincott Company, 1928).

[7] National Science Foundation, *Evolution of Evolution: Flash Special Report Timeline: www.nsf.gov/news/special_reports/darwin/textonly/timeline.jsp* (September 2, 2015).

[8] Keith, 1915, p. 305.

[9] Volume I, *The Antiquity of Man* by Sir Arthur Keith. Philadelphia: J.B. Lippincott Company, 1925. Second Edition, Sixth Impression. Illustrated. Image Credit: *http://www.oakauctions.com/clarence-darrow-signed-%E2%80%9Cthe-antiquity-of-man%E2%80%9D-lot1674.aspx*.

[10] Isabelle De Groote, et al. "New genetic and morphological evidence suggests a single hoaxer created 'Piltdown man,'" *Royal Society Open Science*. 3 (2016).

[11] Image Credit: Wikipedia.

[12] William K. Gregory, "Hesperopithecus Apparently Not an Ape nor a Man," *Science*, 66 (1720) (December 16, 1927): 579–581.

[13] Ralph M. Wetzel, et al., "Catagonus, An 'Extinct' Peccary, Alive in Paraguay," *Science*, 189 (4200) (Aug. 1, 1975): 379.

[14] Duane T. Gish, *Evolution: The Fossils Still Say NO!* (El Cajon, CA: Institute for Creation Research, 1995). p. 328.

[15] Image Credit: This reconstruction of the La Chapelle-aux-Saints Neanderthal skeleton—discovered in France in 1908—was published in *L'Illustration* and in the *Illustrated London News* in 1909.

[16] Image Credit: Wikipedia.

[17] W.L. Jungers, "Lucy's length: Stature reconstruction in Australopithecus afarensis (A.L.288-1) with implications for other small-bodied hominids." *American Journal of Physical Anthropology*. 76 (2) (1988): 227–231.

[18] Some of these fatal flaws pertain to Lucy's actual fossil, some are in regards to how her fossil is represented, and some involve both.

[19] NOVA, *In Search of Human Origins (Part I)* (Airdate: June 3, 1997): *http://www.pbs.org/wgbh/nova/transcripts/2106hum1.html* (September 2, 2015).

[20] Time magazine reported in 1977 that Lucy had a tiny skull, a head like an ape, a braincase size the same as that of a chimp—450 cc. and "was surprisingly short legged" (*Time*, November 7, 1979, pp. 68–69). See also: Smithsonian National Museum of Natural History, "Australopithecus afarensis": *http://humanorigins.si.edu/evidence/human-fossils/species/australopithecus-afarensis* (September 2, 2015).

[21] Solly Zuckerman, *Beyond the Ivory Tower* (London: Taplinger Publishing Company, 1970), p. 78.

[22] Skull from: *www.skullsunlimited.com*

[23] William H. Kimbel and Yoel Rak. "The Cranial Base of Australopithecus Afarensis: New Insights from the Female Skull." *Philosophical Transactions of the Royal Society B: Biological Sciences* 365.1556 (2010): 3365–3376.

[24] Upper Image Credit: M. H. Wolpoff, J. Hawks, B. Senut, M. Pickford, J. Ahern, "An Ape or the Ape: Is the Toumaï Cranium TM 266 a Hominid?" PaleoAnthropology. 2006: 36–50 (upper two images, arrows added). Lower Image Credit: Evolution Facts, Inc. *Evolution Encyclopedia Volume 2, Chapter 18 Ancient Man* (*www.godrules.net/evolutioncruncher/2evlch18a.htm).* (January 27, 2017). FM differences discussed in: William H. Kimbel and Rak Yoel. "The Cranial Base of Australopithecus Afarensis: New Insights from the Female Skull." *Philosophical Transactions of the Royal Society B: Biological Sciences* 365.1556 (2010): 3365–3376.

[25] Ibid., 3369–3370

[26] Image Credit: Wikipedia.

[27] Fred Spoor, Bernard Wood, Frans Zonneveld, "Implications of Early Hominid Labyrinthine Morphology for Evolution of Human Bipedal Locomotion," *Nature* 369 (June 23, 1994): 645–648.

[28] Smithsonian: *http://humanorigins.si.edu/evidence/human-fossils/species/australopithecus-africanus* (January 27, 2017).

[29] Bernard Wood, "A precious little bundle," *Nature* 443, 278–281 (September 21, 2006).

[30] Kate Wong, "Special Report: Lucy's Baby An extraordinary new human fossil comes to light," *Scientific American*: *www.scientificamerican.com/article/special-report-lucys-baby/* (September 20, 2006) (January 27, 2017).

[31] Healthline Bodymaps: *www.healthline.com/human-body-maps/semicircular-canals.* Medically Reviewed on January 26, 2015 by Healthline Medical Team (January 27, 2017).

[32] F. Spoor and F. Zonneveld. "Comparative review of the human bony labyrinth," *Am J Phys Anthropology*, Supplement 27 (1998): 211–51. P. Gunz, et al., "The Mammalian Bony Labyrinth Reconsidered: Introducing a Comprehensive Geometric Morphometric Approach," *Journal of Anatomy* 220, 6 (2012): 529–543.

[33] Fred Spoor, Bernard Wood, Frans Zonneveld, "Implications of Early Hominid Labyrinthine Morphology for Evolution of Human Bipedal Locomotion," *Nature* 369 (June 23, 1994): 645–648.

[34] Brian L. Day, et al. "The vestibular system," *Current Biology*, 15 (15), R583 - R586.

[35] Image Credit: Shutterstock.

[36] Adam Summers, "Born to Run: Humans will Never Win a Sprint against your Average Quadruped. But our Species is well-adapted for the Marathon," *Biomechanics: www.naturalhistorymag.com/biomechanics/112078/born-to-run* (September 1, 2015).

[37] Marc R. Meyer, Scott A. Williams, Michael P. Smith, Gary J. Sawyer, "Lucy's back: Reassessment of fossils associated with the A.L. 288-1 vertebral column," *Journal of Human Evolution*, 85 (August 2015): 174–180.

[38] Personal communication: "All [Lucy's bones were] found in an area covering about 3 square meters." Donald Johanson (May 28, 2014).

[39] *Atlas of Science*, "Archaeological surprise! Lucy has company," *https://atlasofscience.org/archaeological-surprise-lucy/* (November 30, 2015) (January 27, 2017).

[40] PBS Evolution, "Finding Lucy": *www.pbs.org/wgbh/evolution/library/07/1/l_071_01.html* (September 2, 2015).

[41] Ibid.

[42] F. Marchal, "A new morphometric analysis of the hominid pelvic bone," *Journal of Human Evolution*, 38(3) (March 2000): 347–65.

[43] Jack Stern & Randall L. Susman, "The Locomotor Anatomy of Australopithecus afarensis," *Journal of Physical Anthropology* 60 (1983): 291–292.

[44] Charles Oxnard, *The Order of Man: A Biomathematical Anatomy of the Primates* (Yale University Press and Hong Kong University Press, 1984): 3.

[45] Image Credit: *Australopithecus afarensis* (*History Alive! The Ancient World* (Palo Alto, CA: Teachers Curriculum Institute, 2004).

[46] Brian G. Richmond and David S. Strait, "Evidence That Humans Evolved From a Knuckle-Walking Ancestor," *Nature*, 404 (2000): 382–385.

[47] Maggie Fox, "Man's Early Ancestors Were Knuckle Walkers," *San Diego Union Tribune* (Quest Section, March 29, 2000).

[48] Richmond & Strait, *Evidence That Humans Evolved From a Knuckle-Walking Ancestor*, pp. 382–385.

[49] Guy Gugliotta, "It's All in the Wrist Early Human Ancestors Were 'Knuckle-Walkers,' Research Indicates," Washington Post (March 23, 2000), A03.

[50] Richmond & Strait, *Evidence That Humans Evolved From a Knuckle-Walking Ancestor*, pp. 382–385.

[51] Ibid.

[52] Manuel Domínguez-Rodrigo, Travis Rayne Pickering, Sergio Almécija, Jason L. Heaton, Enrique Baquedano, Audax Mabulla & David Uribelarrea, "Earliest modern human-like hand bone from a new >1.84-million-year-old site at Olduvai in Tanzania," *Nature Communications* 6, 7987 (2015); Jack Stern & Randall L. Susman, "The Locomotor Anatomy of Australopithecus afarensis," *Journal of Physical Anthropology* 60 (1983): 280.

[53] Ibid.

[54] Ibid.

[55] Jack Stern & Randall L. Susman, "The Locomotor Anatomy of Australopithecus afarensis," *Journal of Physical Anthropology* 60 (1983): 280.

[56] W. L. Jungers, "Lucy's limbs: skeletal allometry and locomotion in Australopithecus afarensis." *Nature* 297 (1982): 676–678.

[57] Stern & Susman, 1983.

[58] K.D. Hunt, "The evolution of human bipedality: ecology and functional morphology." *Journal of Human Evolution*, 26 (1994): 183–202.

[59] PBS Evolution, "Finding Lucy": *www.pbs.org/wgbh/evolution/library/07/1/l_071_01.html* (September 2, 2015); National Geographic, "What was 'Lucy'? Fast Facts on an Early Human Ancestor" (September 20, 2006). *National Geographic News: http://news.nationalgeographic.com/news/2006/09/060920-lucy.html* (September 2, 2015).

[60] Donald Johanson & Edgar Blake. *From Lucy to Language* (New York: Simon & Schuster, 1996).

[61] Image Credit: Answers in Genesis (left); Brian Thomas (right).

[62] Personal communication: "All [Lucy's bones were] found in an area covering about 3 square meters." Professor Donald Johanson (May 28, 2014).

[63] Licensed through Alamy. Photo Credit Franck Robichon/epa/Corbis.

[64] M. Häusler & P. Schmid, "Comparison of the Pelves of Sts 14 and AL 288-1: Implications for Birth and Sexual Dimorphism in Australopithecines." *Journal of Human Evolution* 29 (1995): 363–383.

[65] Alan Boyle, "Lucy or Brucey? It Can Be Tricky to Tell the Sex of Fossil Ancestors," *Science* (April 29, 2015).

[66] Image Credit: Wikipedia.

[67] Source: *http://news.utexas.edu/2016/08/29/ut-study-cracks-coldest-case-how-lucy-died* (January 27, 2017).

[68] J. Kappelman, R.A. Ketcham, S. Pearce, L. Todd, W. Akins, M.W. Colbert, et al, "Perimortem fractures in Lucy suggest mortality from fall out of tall tree." *Nature*, 537 (September 22, 2016): 503–507. *www.nature.com/nature/journal/v537/n7621/full/nature19332.html*

[69] Oxnard, *The Order of Man: A Biomathematical Anatomy of the Primates*, p. 3.

[70] Roger Lewin, *Bones of Contention* (Chicago: University of Chicago Press, 1987), p. 164.

[71] Wray Herbert, "Lucy's Uncommon Forbear," *Science News* 123 (February 5, 1983), p. 89.

[72] Albert W. Mehlert, "Lucy—Evolution's Solitary Claim for an Ape/Man: Her Position is Slipping Away," *Creation Research Society Quarterly*, 22 (3) (December, 1985), p. 145.

[73] Marvin Lubenow, *Bones of Contention* (Grand Rapids, MI: Baker Books, 1992), p. 179.

[74] DeWitt Steele & Gregory Parker, *Science of the Physical Creation*, 2d ed. (Pensacola, FL: A Beka Book, 1996), p. 299.

[75] "Before humans left Babel, it appears that apes had already spread over much of the Old World and had diversified into a large array of species… Paleontologists are still discovering species of post-Flood apes. If we are correct about post-Flood rocks, apes were at their highest point of diversity and were buried in local catastrophes just before humans spread out from Babel." Kurt Wise, "Lucy Was Buried First Babel Helps Explain the Sequence of Ape and Human Fossils," (August 20, 2008), *Answers in Genesis: https://answersingenesis.org/human-evolution/lucy/lucy-was-buried-first/* (September 2, 2015).

[76] Hugh Ross, "Species Development: Natural Process or Divine Action," Creation and Time Audiotape, Tape 2, Side 1 (Pasadena, CA: Reasons to Believe, 1990).

[77] World Wide Fund for Nature, "What do Pandas eat? The simple answers is: bamboo," Pando.org: *www.wwf.panda.org/what_we_do/endangered_species/giant_panda/panda/what_do_pandas_they_eat/* (February 13, 2017).

[78] Nathaniel T. Jeanson, "Did Lions Roam the Garden of Eden?" ICR.org: *www.icr.org/article/did-lions-roam-garden-eden/* (February 13, 2017).

[79] Overview Eric Hovind and Paul Taylor welcome special guest Dr. G. Charles Jackson in the August 18, 2011 episode of Creation Today.

[80] John MacArthur, "Creation: Believe It or Not, Part 2 (90–209)": *www.gty.org/resources/sermons/90-209/creation-believe-it-or-not-part-2* (March 28, 1999) (January 27, 2017).

[81] Summarized from: Southern Baptist Convention. "How to Become a Christian." *www.sbc.net/knowjesus/theplan.asp.* Accessed March 16, 2016.

Made in the USA
Monee, IL
12 April 2023

31244116R00036